The Legend of

GID
THE KID

AND THE

BLACK BEAN BANDITS

written and illustrated by

THE MILLER BROTHERS

For Toby, Keegan and Henry
The world could use a few more heroes... just like you!

Published by Warner Press Inc   Anderson, IN 46012
www.warnerpress.com

Text ©2007 by Lumination Studios
Illustrations ©2007 by Lumination Studios

ISBN: 1-59317-202-8

Editor: Karen Rhodes
Creative Director: Curtis D. Corzine
Story & 3-D Illustration: Christopher & Allan Miller

LUMINATION
STUDIOS

Printed in Singapore

Warner Press Kids™
educate • nurture • inspire

In those days
there was no sheriff
and everyone did what was right
in his own eyes...

The town of Promise was known through the West
for its black bean chili 'cause it was the best.
But instead of being proud of the award they had won,
they were afraid that one day Bean Bandits would come.

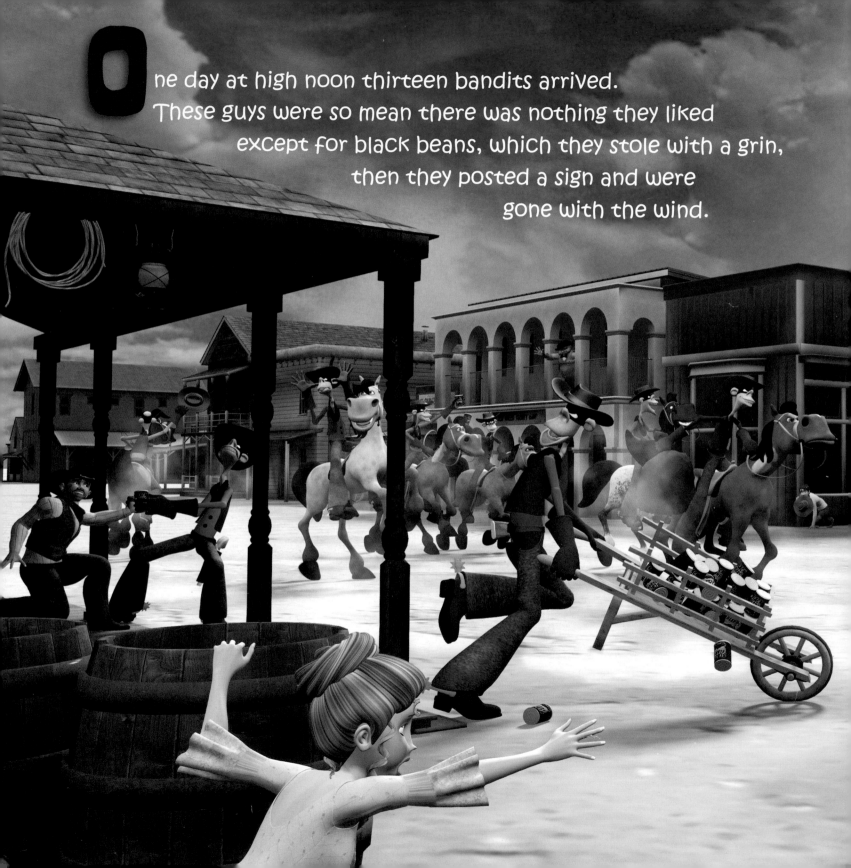

One day at high noon thirteen bandits arrived.
These guys were so mean there was nothing they liked
except for black beans, which they stole with a grin,
then they posted a sign and were
gone with the wind.

Mayor McDoogal was the first to speak up,
"If the White Rider were here, he'd capture those thugs!
What we need is a sheriff to stand up to these dudes!"
No one stepped forward. They all shook in their boots…

The bandits came back
every week to steal lunch.
Young Gid, like the others,
was afraid of the bunch,
so he hid all his beans in
the mines outside town.

"They'll never look here,"
he said glancing around.

"**H**owdy, son!" Out of nowhere a stranger appeared.
"Why are you hiding your beans way out here?
Those Bandits are bullies. Stand up—don't back down.
Now put on this badge and go take back your town!"

Gid was as quick as a freshly made whip.
He didn't trust strangers; it could be a trick.
"I'm no sheriff," Gid said, "I'm too small and too slow.
If you think it's so easy then why don't you go?"

"**I**'m the White Rider," the man said with a wink, "and when I ride with you, you're more brave than you think." Gid paused for a moment; could it really be true? "If you are who you say, show me what you can do!"

The Rider laughed warmly, then said something silly.
"I have an idea; bring a cold pot of chili."
Then he narrowed his eyes and with a tip of his hat
a fire burst under Gid's pot, just like that!

"That's a pretty slick trick." Gid turned in surprise,
but the Rider was gone. Gid just rubbed his eyes...

Then a voice in the sky said, "Stand up for what's right.
Don't be afraid, I'll help in the fight!
And don't forget, eat your chili while it's still hot tonight!"

Early next morning the town gathered 'round...
where the sign had once been was a hole in the ground!
"When the bandits come back they'll be angry with us!
Who could have done this?" they wondered and fussed.

"I did!" Gid stated, as he stood proud and tall.
With the badge on his chest he didn't feel quite as small.
"Get him!" the mob shouted and started to charge,
but the mayor stepped in before Gid could be harmed.

"Whose side are ya'll on? We're not like the bandits!
If Gid has something to say let's not misunderstand it.
Now let's hear the boy out before we decide."
Then Gid gave the challenge to stand up, not to hide!

"The White Rider is back," Gid explained to the crowd,
"and he rides along side us to take back our town!"
"Hooray!" the town shouted, "The Rider's alive!"
And twenty-one men saddled up for the ride.

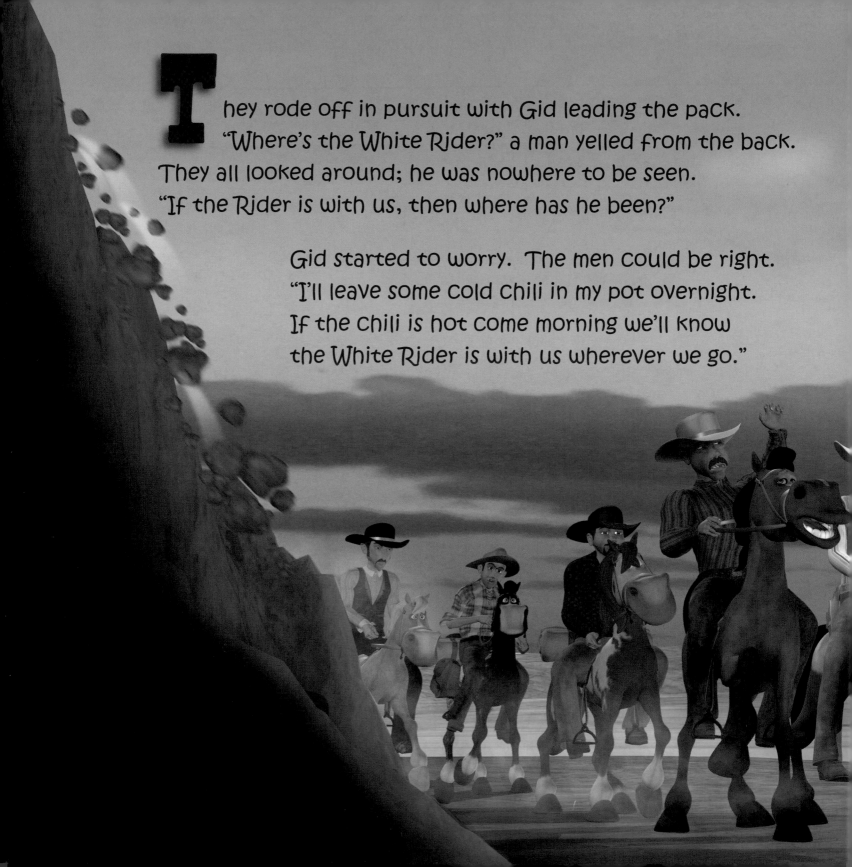

They rode off in pursuit with Gid leading the pack.
"Where's the White Rider?" a man yelled from the back.
They all looked around; he was nowhere to be seen.
"If the Rider is with us, then where has he been?"

Gid started to worry. The men could be right.
"I'll leave some cold chili in my pot overnight.
If the chili is hot come morning we'll know
the White Rider is with us wherever we go."

The smell of black beans woke Gid up on the spot;
the White Rider was there and the chili was hot.
"Howdy, son." The White Rider sat tending the fire.
"Looks like a mighty big posse you've hired."

"In fact it's too many, countin' me on your side.
Send home every man who has fear in his eyes!"
Gid needed the men but agreed it was best.
When the dust finally settled...
just seven were left.

"**S**even's too many, I think you'll agree,"
the Rider declared, "we'll need only three!
Keep only the most alert of your clan—
the ones who eat black beans straight from the can!"

"Only three men against more than a dozen?
You must be mistaken!" Gid's head was a-buzzin'.
But the Rider convinced him the Law would prevail,
so only two men rode with Gid down the trail.

Up 'round the bend they could see Devil's Bluff
where the Bean Bandits camped with their chili and stuff.
"We'll set up an ambush and take them by surprise.
Split up, surround them, take cover and hide."

When the glow of the moon peeked out from a cloud
Gid's men banged their pots and they shouted out loud,
"Bean Bandits beware—the White Rider is here!
As long as he's with us we've nothing to fear!"

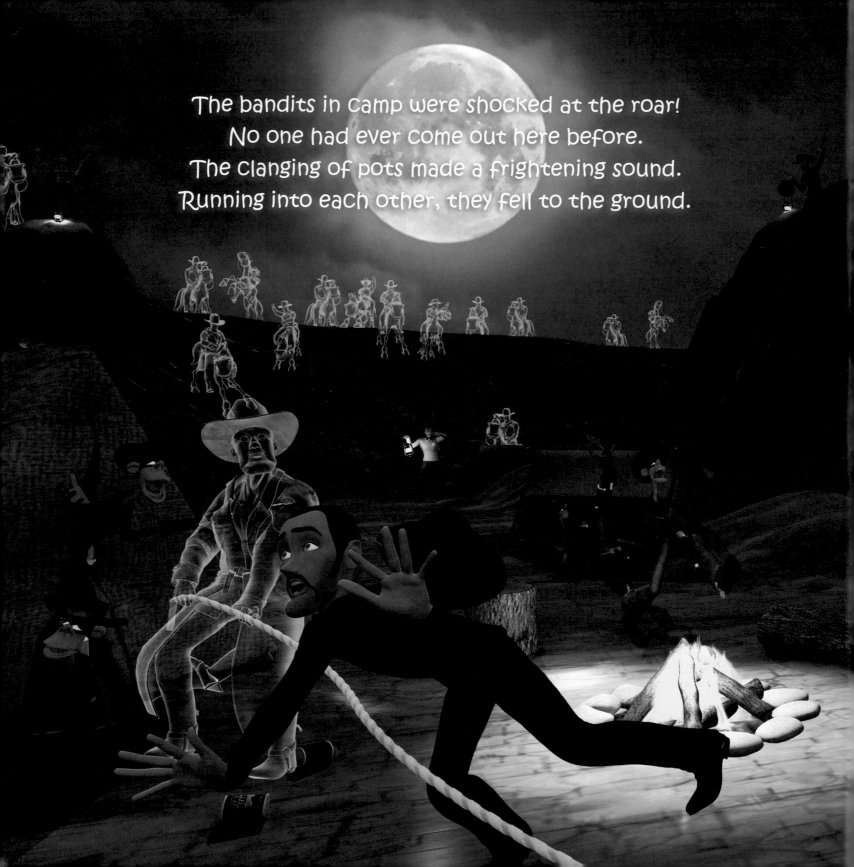

The bandits in camp were shocked at the roar!
No one had ever come out here before.
The clanging of pots made a frightening sound.
Running into each other, they fell to the ground.

The victors rode home with the bandits in tow.
The town threw a party like none they had known.
"Three cheers for our Gid," the proud mayor raved.
"He trusted the Rider and our town has been saved."

So the people of Promise learned a lesson that day.
When bullies do bad things don't be afraid.
Stand up for what's right; don't hide back in fear.
Just trust the White Rider, he'll always be near...
and remember, black bean chili goes great with root beer.

The End

Ponderin' Points

Just like Gid, you probably know people in your life who do mean things and act like bullies. Here are some questions to talk about with your family.

- Is it okay for people to do mean things? Why not?

- What do you think is the best way to deal with bullies?

- If we let people do mean things will the world be a safer place to live?

- Who do you think the White Rider represents in this story?

- How did the White Rider help Gid?

- Do things always go smoothly when we confront bad people?

- If bad things happen when we do the right thing should we stop doing what is right?

The Roundup

Albert Einstein once said, "The world is a dangerous place, not because of those who do evil, but because of those who look on and do nothing." That means we need good people to stand up for what's right (even when it's scary) in order to stop people from being mean.

For the truth behind the legend check out the true story of Gideon in your Bible (Judges 6:11—7:25).

BEST IN THE WEST
BLACK BEAN CHILI

To print this recipe visit www.HeroesOfPromise.com

- 1 pound Ground Beef (browned & drained)
- 1/2 large Onion, diced
- 2 teaspoons Cumin
- 1 10 oz Can Diced Tomatoes with Green Chilies
- 1 15 oz Can Tomato Sauce
- 1/4 teaspoon Salt
- 2 15 oz Cans Black Beans, drained, but reserve liquid
- 1 tablespoon Sugar
- 1/2 cup Liquid from Beans

Cooking Directions:

1. Brown meat. Drain and add onion, cumin and salt.
2. Add tomatoes, tomato sauce and sugar. Cook until warm all the way through.
3. Add beans and liquid and cook for 3-5 minutes.

Don't overcook or beans will get mushy. Serve with cheese and sour cream.

DID YOU KNOW ?

We have hidden 24 geckos throughout this book. Think you found them all? Visit www.HeroesOfPromise.com to find out.